Oracle Tables, Clusters and Partitions

ARUN KUMAR

Oracle Tables, Clusters and Partitions

Copyright © 2019 by Arun Kumar

Founder and Instructor at DBA Genesis


```
Note: All the queries in this book will look like
this format.
```

For any queries, write to support@dbagenesis.com

DEDICATION

I would like to dedicate this book to my family, who has been always there for me whenever I need

ACKNOWLEDGEMENT

Your comments encourage us to produce quality content, please take a second and say 'Hi' to me and let me and my team know what you thought of the book … p.s. It would mean the world to me if you send a quick email to me ;)

Email: support@dbagenesis.com

- Link to full course: https://dbagenesis.com/
- Link to all DBA courses: https://dbagenesis.com/courses
- Link to real-time projects: https://dbagenesis.com/p/projects
- Link to support articles: https://support.dbagenesis.com

All the best and I hope you enjoy this book!

Arun Kumar

Table of Content

CHAPTER 1

Database Schema and Objects

Table

In a database, the basic storage unit that we called it as a table. All the tables inside the database make one big database.

What are all the objects inside a database that actually takes space?

Tables are one of those objects which occupy disk space inside the database. Apart from tables, indexes that Oracle creates for you those are all also object that take space on disk.

Only two objects inside the entire database take the disk space that are table and index.

What is the difference between Database user and Schema?

Database User

In real time, there are multiple users for any application. But inside the database, user will never map to a real-time person. You cannot have a User = Customer, User = Builder or User = Owner of the business. Inside the database, user maps to an application user. That application can be used by N number of people that can again be the customer itself or call center person who is helping you.

An application that speaks with database, that application will have only one user, that user will be in common and used by end customers / users. Always inside the database, when you create a user, it must be an application user. It should not be mapped to any real time user. All the uses inside the database must be created based on the application rules, not based on the real time users.

- Database user are different from OS users
- DB user and OS user can be same
- User are created by CREATE USER statements
- Schema is a user in database who owns at least one object
- Each user owns a single schema
- Schema name is same as username
- Example, HR user owns HR schema
- DB user has password and privileges
- In production, schema owner represents a database application rather than a person

If you create some objects inside the database, then you call it as a schema. A user will be called as schema if it owns at least one object inside a database. Schema name will be exactly the same as the user name. You cannot have multiple schemas which are assigned to one username.

DB user has password and privileges. The password and privileges are given to DB user and after that again drill down to password and privileges to schema. In production, schema owner represents a database application rather than a person.

Schema Object

Schema and User, these two terms will be used vice-versa because they are very close. Schema objects are the user objects, these are the objects that can be owned or have access to the user. Each object has a unique name referred as **schema_name.object_name**.

- Each object has unique name referred as schema_name.object_name
- HR.EMPLOYEE refers to employee table owned by HR schema
- Shema owns different types of DB objects like:
  - Tables
  - Indexes
  - Partitions
  - Views
  - Sequences etc
- All schema objects are stored in data files

HR.EMPLOYEE refers to employee table owned by the HR schema. When we write HR.EMPLOYEE, it simply refers to the employee table which is owned by the HR schema.

Schema owns different types of DB objects like:

- Tables
- Indexes
- Partitions
- Views
- Sequences

All schema objects are stored in data files.

How do we check the table inside the database?

You can always query DBA_TABLES or DBA_OBJECTS to view all the tables or objects inside the database.

```
SQL> dba_tables;
SP2-0042: unknown command "dba_tables" - rest of line ignored.
SQL>
SQL>
SQL> desc dba_tables;
```

```
MAX_EXTENTS                         NUMBER
PCT_INCREASE                        NUMBER
FREELISTS                           NUMBER
FREELIST_GROUPS                     NUMBER
LOGGING                             VARCHAR2 (3)
BACKED_UP                           VARCHAR2 (1)
NUM_ROWS                            NUMBER
BLOCKS                              NUMBER
EMPTY_BLOCKS                        NUMBER
AVG_SPACE                           NUMBER
CHAIN_CNT                           NUMBER
AVG_ROW_LEN                         NUMBER
AVG_SPACE_FREELIST_BLOCKS           NUMBER
NUM_FREELIST_BLOCKS                 NUMBER
DEGREE                              VARCHAR2 (10)
INSTANCES                           VARCHAR2 (10)
CACHE                               VARCHAR2 (5)
TABLE_LOCK                          VARCHAR2 (8)
SAMPLE_SIZE                         NUMBER
LAST_ANALYZED                       DATE
PARTITIONED                         VARCHAR2 (3)
IOT_TYPE                            VARCHAR2 (12)
TEMPORARY                           VARCHAR2 (1)
SECONDARY                           VARCHAR2 (1)
NESTED                              VARCHAR2 (3)
BUFFER_POOL                         VARCHAR2 (7)
FLASH_CACHE                         VARCHAR2 (7)
CELL_FLASH_CACHE                    VARCHAR2 (7)
ROW_MOVEMENT                        VARCHAR2 (8)
GLOBAL_STATS                        VARCHAR2 (3)
USER_STATS                          VARCHAR2 (3)
DURATION                            VARCHAR2 (15)
SKIP_CORRUPT                        VARCHAR2 (8)
```

If you want to see all the objects, then we need to use the below query:

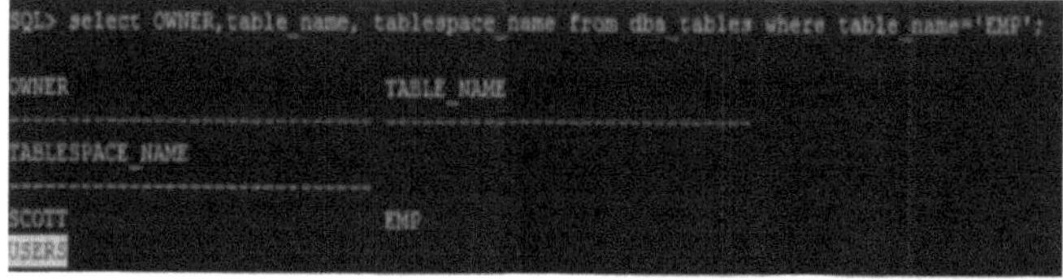

Suppose we want to see who is the owner of the table & do we have multiple tables inside the database with the name EMP

The above out shows, its own by scott user and the table name is EMP.

CHAPTER 2

Tables in Database

Table is the building structures of the database. And, this is the only apart from indexes which takes the physical space.

- Basic unit of data storage in rows and columns
- Tables are permanent or temporary
- Table columns consists of data and have specific data type
- Each table is added with rowid column
- Rowid is a physical address of each row
- Rowid is used in indexes to refer rows physical
- You can give partial or full privileges on tables to other users in database

Tables are the basic unit of data storage in the form of rows and columns. And you have multiple columns where you have multiple rows inside it. Sometimes column is also called as attribute and rows are also called as tuples.

There are two types of tables inside the database:

- Permanent tables
- Temporary tables

What are the temporary tables?

When you perform sorting in your query, it will create some temporary tables where it can perform the sorting. Those are called as temporary tables because, they can be flushed out and they can be overwritten by oracle itself.

Thats why, inside the temporary tablespace nothing will be permanent. Once Shutdown the database everything will be flushed out and once you start the database you have a clean temporary tablespace.

It can be considered as RAM because in RAM, we also have all the contents but once you shut down and restart the system, there won't be anything in the RAM.

Table columns consists of data and have specific data type. To distinguish the data inside the table, every column is assigned with the data type. It will help Oracle understand what kind of data or what nature of data is coming inside a column.

Each table is added with row ID column. When you create a table inside the database, row ID column will be created. It's a Hidden column.

Row ID will have the physical address of each row. Physical address means where exactly the rows stored.

Row ID is used in indexes to refer rows physically. When you query any table or data inside the table, Oracle will check if there is an index to the any specific column. If the index column is included inside your WHERE clause, then it will use index, directly pickup the row ID from the index and throw the output.

You can give partial or full privileges on tables to other users inside the database. We have different tables inside the database and in case if you want to grant permission to others, you can give a select, delete, update or may be all permissions to other users inside the database depending on the application requirement.

CHAPTER 3

Table Cluster

Cluster is one big table containing multiple small tables. You can create a Cluster and you can put all the tables inside the cluster which share one single column which is like a primary key or a foreign key among all the tables.

You cannot put tables which do not share a single common column or which you consider it as a cluster key.

- A cluster is one big table containing multiple small tables
- Each table inside cluster have common column(s)
- The common column(s) is called as cluster key
- Cluster key must be specified during cluster table creations
- Clustering of tables should be done when they are primarily queried NOT MODIFIED
- Disk I/O is reduced in cluster tables
- Access time improves for joining of cluster tables

Each table inside cluster have common columns(s)

Each table inside cluster will have common column, that can be one single column or there can be multiple columns which are considered as primary key or a foreign key. Because of a table is small or we have an employee and department table, we have only one common column that is Department number.

But in real time you can have something called as Composite keys. It means having more than one column inside the key column. That's why each table inside cluster have common column or columns depending on the composite key. Because in real time, you have big tables and big tables will have multiple keys and in those keys, there can be single key or composite key.

The common column(s) inside a cluster is called as Cluster key

Depending on the key of the primary key or foreign key, those will become the cluster key. In general the columns on which all the tables are joined are called as cluster key.

Cluster key must be specified during cluster table creations

When you create a cluster, you need to specify the key column. Otherwise, when you try to add the tables, if you do not specify the key column matching to the cluster key, it won't take the table. So when you create the cluster itself, you need to specify the key column.

Clustering of tables should be done when they are primarily queried NOT MODIFIED

You should only cluster tables when you know that a query will come to only select the data and not modify the table. Because it becomes very DBS inside the clustering or it will impact the performance. When you try to modify the data inside a cluster is very easy to just query the data of cluster.

It is not suggested to create clusters when you have more number of alter or updates or delete. You can have a cluster when you have a lot of select statement and all the select having lot of joints on two common tables. That time it's advisable to go for cluster.

Disk I/O is reduced in cluster tables

When we have a table cluster, it will definitely reduce the desk I/O and that's when your database performance will increase.

Access time improves for joining of cluster tables

When you try to join the tables inside the cluster, the access time will increase because everything resides into one big cluster or at one place.

CHAPTER 4

Creating a Cluster Table

Let us create an index cluster on employees and department table under scott user:

Create cluster table

```
SQL>
SQL>
SQL> CREATE CLUSTER employees_departments_cluster
(department_id NUMBER(2));   2

Cluster created.
```

Create index on cluster table

Without creating an index on cluster table, you cannot proceed. This is an Index Cluster.

```
SQL>
SQL> CREATE INDEX idx_emp_dept_cluster ON CLUSTER employees_departments_cluster;

Index created.
```

Create table inside cluster based on cluster key column

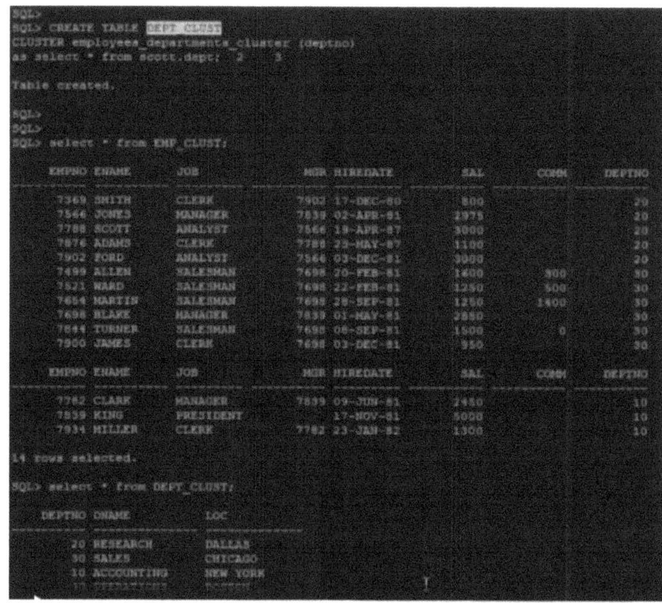

Create a second table inside cluster

Now we are going to create a second table DEPT_CLUST inside the same CLUSTER and then see how to query tables from a CLUSTER

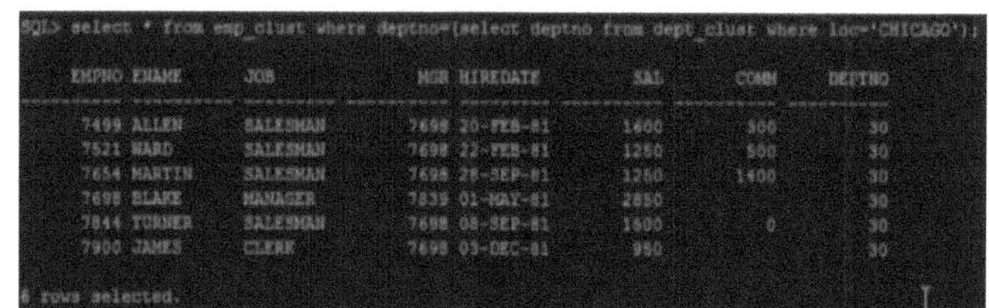

Dropping a table inside the cluster

Drop the entire cluster

```
SQL>
SQL> DROP CLUSTER employees_departments_cluster;

Cluster dropped.
```

How Tables Cluster look inside the database

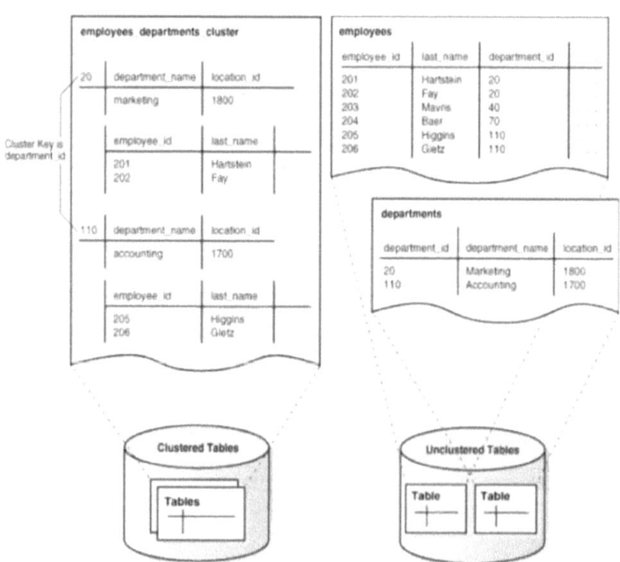

When you have two tables i.e. an employee and department stored separately even though you have a department ID column which is joining tables, database will store both the table separately. And, when you query any table or any join query, it will get the data of those two physical locations where the tables are stored.

employees_departments_cluster

20	department_name	location_id	
	marketing	1800	
	employee_id	last_name	
	201	Hartstein	
	202	Fay	

Cluster Key is department_id

But when it comes to the cluster, you have the key column and rows are stored from both the tables. As we can see in the above cluster table picture, we have an employee and department table both are joined with their department ID. The department ID 20, department_name is Marketing department and there are only two employee IDs, 201 and 202 which belong to department #20.

110	department_name	location_id	
	accounting	1700	
	employee_id	last_name	
	205	Higgins	
	206	Gietz	

We have the departmentID 110, department_name is accounting and accounting department is having only two people, 205 and 206 as we see in the above picture.

When it comes to cluster table, key column will be mentioned first i.e. 20. This key column will contain the rows which are mapped to the department in one single area.

When we query where department ID=20, now records from department table and employee table are stored at one location, the retrieval or the access time will be very fast.

Same thing goes with 110 departmentID, you have the accounting department, location ID and you also have all the employees which belong to the 110 department.

That's how rather than physically getting the data from two different tables, everything is now stored in one big table at OS level i.e. cluster and everything is at one place.

With each department or the key column, you have the record from both the tables. So it becomes easy to pull out the data at one shot, when you refer to the key columns. That is the way Cluster work inside the database.

CHAPTER 6

Tables and Index Partition overview

When you have one single table, it makes more sense to create partitions than to access the entire table. Because accessing smaller partitions becomes easier for Oracle than accessing one big table.

Example:

There is an office and in the office everything is kept into separate boxes. Let's take the office is trying to shift from one place to another place. It makes more sense to keep everything into smaller boxes and then you move the small boxes rather than keeping everything into a one big box and then you try to move that box out of the premises. So it's always good to have everything divided and in that sense it becomes easy and it's always manageable to move things around.

- Enables easy data manageability
- Very large tables are very hard to manage
- Partitioning allows to create smaller tables or indexes
- Each partition is an independent object
- Each partition has its own name and storage characteristics
- Unavailability of one partition does not affect other
- Each partition must have same columns
- Each partition can reside in different tablespaces

Enables easy data manageability

It will enable you to manage the data very easily, because your data is now stored in small chunks rather than one very big table.

This partitioning concept is actually almost reverse of table clustering. Table clustering is integration. You joining or combining two tables into one big table i.e clustering. Table partitioning is kind of like dividing.

Very large tables are very hard to manage

When we say very hard to manage, it doesn't mean Oracle is not capable of managing them. It just means that the performance is hit even if you have a very big table and you have the indexes, still your select will take a lot of time. Because there is a lot of rows that your index has to scan.

Even if you have very big table and you are ok with the query response, there is no need to go for partitions. But if you go for partitions of very large tables, it will definitely increase the performance to a greater degree.

Partitioning allows to create smaller tables or indexes!

Why do we say tables and index partitions?

Because these are the only two objects which take disk space inside a database. That's why you have tables which will take the disk space, you have indexes which will take the disk space. These two terms index and tables are jointly used.

You need to have index assigned to some table or some column and that's the reason you have a table. When you partition the table, 1 index will also be partitioned because indexes also attached to a table.

When it comes to indexes, it's not needed to partition indexes but in case if you want then you can do it.

Each partition is an independent object

When we say independent object in a normal database, any object can be placed into any tablespace where the user is having access. Which means if a partition is independent, then a user can place the partition into a different tablespace as well.

Each partition has its own name and storage characteristics

Every partition will have a separate name. You can access or address any partition directly by its name. It's like every table has its own name. Similarly every partition inside the table will have its own name.

Storage characteristics means as we know every partition can be stored on to any tablespace where the user is having access. Which means every partition will have a unique name and also it will have its own characteristics where user has the ability to store them on two different tablespaces.

Unavailability of one partition does not affect another

Let's take entire table is there, and if a table is not available or there is an issue with some part of the table, the entire table won't be available. That is one issue while you have very big table.

If there is an issue with one partition which is stored on some tablespace and there is an issue with that tablespace, you still have the other partitions online. If somebody is querying the data which resides on the other partitions (which are online), the user still gets the answer. That's why the partitions are again become more important and most sensible and very large tables.

Each partition must have same columns

This is something like you can't have different columns or some other type of data inside different partitions. A partition is like a small part or small chunk which is created out of one big table. Those partitions can be placed into different tablespaces. These partitions will have the same number of columns as the main table.

Each partition can reside in different tablespaces

Yes you have a choice to keep all the partitions in two different tablespaces.

CHAPTER 7

Partition Strategy

Partition Strategy means **what strategy can I follow to perform the partitions inside the database**. There are 3 common partition strategies:

1. Range Partition
2. List Partition
3. Hash Partition

There are multiple partitioning strategies like in common, there are three partitioning strategies, but only one will be used everywhere it's the Range partitioning.

It's not easy to manage the partitions or it also needs a special attention of DBA when an environment is having partitions. The range partition is something that is used in very large tables because the data is divided or partition based on the range.

Range Partition

In range partition, database map rows to different partitions based on the partition key. This is the most common type of partitioning strategy. This is used only in the history database is where you are trying to store data for the past.

Basically range partitioning; the word itself will say that you will divide the big table into different partitions based on date range.

List Partition

Database uses a list of values from partition key column to create partition. List partition is like categories. Suppose we have the product categories, we can have one product category into one list and another product category into another list partition. Whenever the data is coming into the product table, it will be judged on the basis of the category that it follows, then depending on the category it will be pushed onto the particular partition.

Hash Partition

Hash is an algorithm that is defined by the user. Actually user doesn't define anything, user will just use the keyword called Hash. Internally Oracle will decide where to place the record.

In hash partitioning, Oracle will distribute the records to all the partition frequently.

Suppose in Hash partition we are having two tables i.e. table one is having 10 records and table two is having 11 records. Oracle will inserted to the table one and making it eleven as we in the below picture:

So this makes sure that data or records are evenly distributed among the partitions inside the table. Inside hash partitioning everything is in control by the database.

List and Hash partition are very least used. The highly used partition is the Range partition.

CHAPTER 8

Range Partition

Range partitioning is the one which is highly used concept and the below diagram is the example for range partitioning.

Example:

Table Partition SALES_1998

PROD_ID	CUST_ID	TIME_ID	CHANNEL_ID	PROMO_ID	QUANTITY_SOLD	AMOUNT_SOLD
40	100530	30-NOV-98	9	33	1	44.99
125	9417	04-FEB-98	3	999	1	16.86
45	9491	28-AUG-98	4	350	1	47.45

Table Partition SALES_1999

PROD_ID	CUST_ID	TIME_ID	CHANNEL_ID	PROMO_ID	QUANTITY_SOLD	AMOUNT_SOLD
116	11393	05-JUN-99	2	999	1	12.18
36	4523	27-JAN-99	3	999	1	53.89
24	11899	26-JUN-99	4	999	1	43.04

We have partition on sales table. This example shows there are two partitions, the first partition is having the records where the sales happened in the year 1998 and the second one is having all the records where the sales happened in the year 1999.

You can literally have partition on any range column where there is a change in the degree. Let it be any numeric column or maybe any time column. Unlike with the year range, you can also have the partition based on the month as well or maybe quarter or half yearly partition depending on the requirement.

Partition Indexes

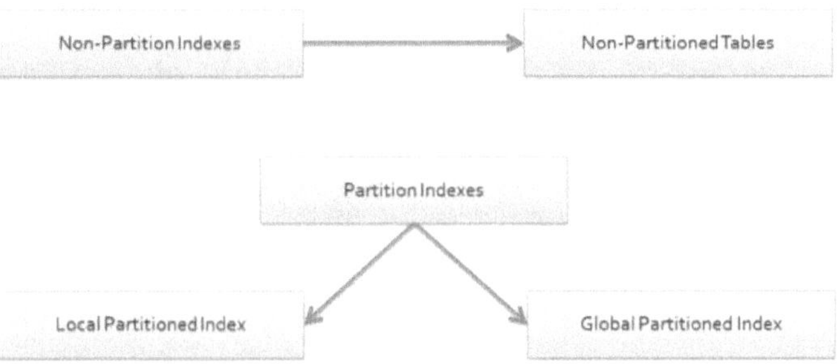

As we talk about partitioning tables, definitely there will be an impact on the indexes as well because indexes are associated with tables. When there is a non partitioned tables, then there will be non partitioned indexes. This is one to one relationship where we have a normal table and a normal table is associated with the normal index.

When we have partition tables, definitely indexes will also be partitioned because indexes are associated with tables.

There are two types of partition indexes inside Oracle database:
1. Local partitioned index
2. Global partitioned index

Local Partitioned Index

Local partitioned index means every partition will have its own index. Whenever somebody queries on the employee table, Oracle will identify in which partition or what is the range of the data.

Because range partitioning is used or when the employee was hired. Depending on the hire date, it will go and check into the particular partition. From there it will use the local index. First it will identify which partition and then it will use the local index of the partition to pull out the record.

Global Partitioned Index

Global partitioned index is one big index which contains details of all the partitions and the records inside those partitions. Global index will work when a query is coming, Oracle will check if it's a partition table. If it's a partition table, then it will first go to the Global index. Inside the Global index, it will identify which partition the data is and where the row is. Then it will go and physically pick up the data from the particular partition and give the output to the user.

Generally people will go with local partitioned indexes because it definitely improves the performance.

CHAPTER 9

Table Partition

Creating the Table Partition

```
CREATE TABLE time_range_sales
   ( prod_id        NUMBER(6) primary key
   , cust_id        NUMBER
   , time_id        DATE
   , quantity_sold  NUMBER(3)
   , amount_sold    NUMBER(10,2)
   )
PARTITION BY RANGE (time_id)
      (PARTITION       SALES_1998       VALUES       LESS       THAN
(TO_DATE('01-JAN-1999','DD-MON-YYYY')) tablespace users,
          PARTITION       SALES_1999       VALUES       LESS       THAN
(TO_DATE('01-JAN-2000','DD-MON-YYYY')) tablespace examples,
          PARTITION       SALES_2000       VALUES       LESS       THAN
(TO_DATE('01-JAN-2001','DD-MON-YYYY')) tablespace xyz,
  PARTITION SALES_2001 VALUES LESS THAN (MAXVALUE) tablespace abc
 );
```

Query to Check Partitions

```
COLUMN high_value FORMAT A20
SELECT table_name,
       partition_name,
       high_value,
       num_rows
FROM   user_tab_partitions
ORDER BY table_name, partition_name;
```

```
SQL> COLUMN high_value FORMAT A20
SELECT table_name,
       partition_name,
       high_value,
       num_rows
FROM   user_tab_partitions
ORDER BY table_name, partition_name;SQL>  2    3    4    5    6
```

```
TABLE_NAME                PARTITION_NAME            HIGH_VALUE             NUM_ROWS
------------------------- ------------------------- -------------------- ----------
TIME_RANGE_SALES          SALES_1998                TO_DATE(' 1999-01-01
                                                     00:00:00', 'SYYYY-M
                                                    M-DD HH24:MI:SS', 'N
                                                    LS_CALENDAR=GREGORIA

TIME_RANGE_SALES          SALES_1999                TO_DATE(' 2000-01-01
                                                     00:00:00', 'SYYYY-M
                                                    M-DD HH24:MI:SS', 'N
                                                    LS_CALENDAR=GREGORIA

TIME_RANGE_SALES          SALES_2000                TO_DATE(' 2001-01-01
TABLE_NAME                PARTITION_NAME            HIGH_VALUE             NUM_ROWS
------------------------- ------------------------- -------------------- ----------
                                                     00:00:00', 'SYYYY-M
                                                    M-DD HH24:MI:SS', 'N
                                                    LS_CALENDAR=GREGORIA

TIME_RANGE_SALES          SALES_2001                MAXVALUE
```

Query the Partition Tables to View Data

```
select * from TIME_RANGE_SALES partition (SALES_1998);
```

```
SQL>
SQL> select * from TIME_RANGE_SALES partition (SALES_1998);

   PROD_ID    CUST_ID TIME_ID   QUANTITY_SOLD AMOUNT_SOLD
---------- ---------- --------- ------------- -----------
       116      11393 05-JUN-99             1         100
        40     100530 30-NOV-98             1         200
       118        133 06-JUN-01             2         300
        36       4523 27-JAN-99             1         500
       125       9417 04-FEB-98             1         600
        30        170 23-FEB-01             1         700
        24      11899 26-JAN-99             1         800
        45       9491 28-AUG-98             1         100

8 rows selected.
```

```
select * from TIME_RANGE_SALES partition (SALES_1999);
```

```
SQL>
SQL> select * from TIME_RANGE_SALES partition (SALES_1999);

no rows selected
```

select * from TIME_RANGE_SALES partition (SALES_2000);

```
SQL>
SQL> select * from TIME_RANGE_SALES partition (SALES_2000);

   PROD_ID    CUST_ID TIME_ID    QUANTITY_SOLD AMOUNT_SOLD
---------- ---------- --------- ------------- -----------
       133       9450 01-DEC-00             1         400
        35       2606 17-FEB-00             1         900
```

Select * from TIME_RANGE_SALES partition (SALES_2001);

```
SQL>
SQL> select * from TIME_RANGE_SALES partition (SALES_2001);

no rows selected
```

Query Entire Partition Table

select * from TIME_RANGE_SALES;

Creating Local Index on Partition Table

```
CREATE INDEX time_range_sales_indx ON TIME_RANGE_SALES(time_id) LOCAL
  (PARTITION year_1 TABLESPACE users,
   PARTITION year_2 TABLESPACE users,
   PARTITION year_3 TABLESPACE users,
   PARTITION year_4 TABLESPACE users);
```

```
SQL> CREATE INDEX time_range_sales_indx ON TIME_RANGE_SALES(time_id) LOCAL
  (PARTITION year_1 TABLESPACE users,
   PARTITION year_2 TABLESPACE users,
   PARTITION year_3 TABLESPACE users,
   PARTITION year_4 TABLESPACE users);  2    3    4    5

Index created.
```

Check Partition Indexes

Syntax:

select INDEX_OWNER,INDEX_NAME,PARTITION_NAME from user_ind_partitions;

```
SQL> select INDEX_OWNER,INDEX_NAME,PARTITION_NAME from all_ind_partitions;

INDEX_OWNER                    INDEX_NAME                   PARTITION_NAME
------------                   ----------                   --------------
AKSGOLU                        GLOB_TIME_RANGE_SALES        GLOB_Y3
AKSGOLU                        GLOB_TIME_RANGE_SALES        GLOB_Y1
AKSGOLU                        GLOB_TIME_RANGE_SALES        GLOB_Y2
AKSGOLU                        GLOB_TIME_RANGE_SALES        GLOB_Y4
```

Create Global Index on Partition Table

Syntax:

```
CREATE INDEX glob_time_range_sales ON TIME_RANGE_SALES(time_id)
GLOBAL PARTITION BY RANGE (time_id)
        (PARTITION          glob_y1        VALUES        LESS        THAN
(TO_DATE('01-JAN-1999','DD-MON-YYYY')),
            PARTITION        glob_y2        VALUES        LESS        THAN
(TO_DATE('01-JAN-2000','DD-MON-YYYY')),
            PARTITION        glob_y3        VALUES        LESS        THAN
(TO_DATE('01-JAN-2001','DD-MON-YYYY')),
   PARTITION glob_y4 VALUES LESS THAN (MAXVALUE));
```

```
SQL> CREATE INDEX glob_time_range_sales ON TIME_RANGE_SALES(time_id)
GLOBAL PARTITION BY RANGE (time_id)
  (PARTITION glob_y1 VALUES LESS THAN (TO_DATE('01-JAN-1999','DD-MON-YYYY')),
   PARTITION glob_y2 VALUES LESS THAN (TO_DATE('01-JAN-2000','DD-MON-YYYY')),
   PARTITION glob_y3 VALUES LESS THAN (TO_DATE('01-JAN-2001','DD-MON-YYYY')),
   PARTITION glob_y4 VALUES LESS THAN (MAXVALUE));  2    3    4    5    6

Index created.
```

Check Partition Indexes

Syntax:

```
select INDEX_NAME,PARTITION_NAME from user_ind_partitions;
```

```
SQL>
SQL> select INDEX_NAME,PARTITION_NAME from user_ind_partitions;

INDEX_NAME                     PARTITION_NAME
----------                     --------------
GLOB_TIME_RANGE_SALES          GLOB_Y1
GLOB_TIME_RANGE_SALES          GLOB_Y2
GLOB_TIME_RANGE_SALES          GLOB_Y3
GLOB_TIME_RANGE_SALES          GLOB_Y4
```

CHAPTER 10

Partitioning Existing Non-Partition Table

There are two ways to achieve it:

1. Take export of table, drop it, create new partition table and then import
2. Use split and exchange partition

Method 1: Take Table Export and Create New Partition Table

Query to check if a Table is Partitioned or Not

```
SQL> select TABLE_NAME,CLUSTER_NAME,PARTITIONED from user_tables;
```

```
SQL> select TABLE_NAME,CLUSTER_NAME,PARTITIONED from user_tables;

TABLE_NAME                          CLUSTER_NAME              PAR
----------------------------------- ------------------------ ---
TIME_RANGE_SALES                                             YES
SALES_TEST                          I                        NO
```

```
SQL> select * from sales_new;
```

```
PROD_ID    CUST_ID TIME_ID  QUANTITY_ SOLD AMOUNT_SOLD
---------- ---------- --------- ------------- -------------------------------------
   116        11393 05-JUN-99        1            100
    40       100530 30-NOV-98        1            200
```

118	33 06-JUN-01	2	300
36	4523 27-JAN-99	1	500
125	9417 04-FEB-98	1	600
30	170 23-FEB-01	1	700
24	11899 26-JAN-99	1	800
45	9491 28-AUG-98	1	100
133	9450 01-DEC-00	1	400
35	606 17-FEB-00	1	900

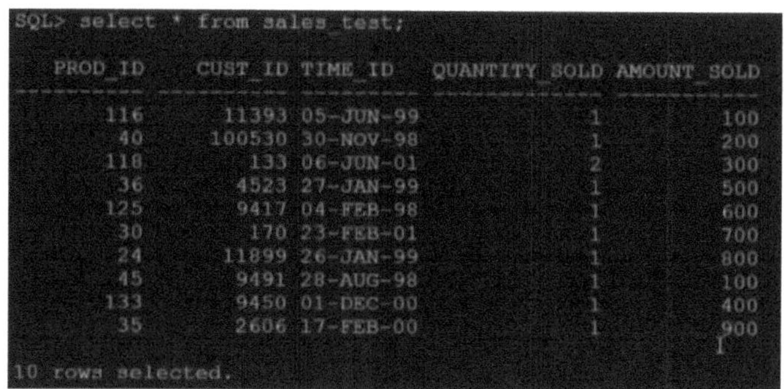

```
SQL> select * from sales_test;

    PROD_ID    CUST_ID TIME_ID   QUANTITY_SOLD AMOUNT_SOLD
---------- ---------- --------- ------------- -----------
       116      11393 05-JUN-99             1         100
        40     100530 30-NOV-98             1         200
       118        133 06-JUN-01             2         300
        36       4523 27-JAN-99             1         500
       125       9417 04-FEB-98             1         600
        30        170 23-FEB-01             1         700
        24      11899 26-JAN-99             1         800
        45       9491 28-AUG-98             1         100
       133       9450 01-DEC-00             1         400
        35       2606 17-FEB-00             1         900

10 rows selected.
```

Take data pump export of the sales table:

```
# exp file=sales_new.exp tables=sales_new

[oracle@ahmed ~]$ ls -lrt
total 20
drwxr-xr-x 3 oracle oinstall  4096 Mar 10 13:21 oradiag_oracle
-rw-r--r-- 1 oracle oinstall 16384 Mar 11 03:20 sales_new.exp
```

Rename the Original Table

```
SQL> rename sales_test to sales_test_bkp;
```

```
SQL> rename sales_test to sales_test_bkp;

Table renamed.
```

Create New Partition Table

```
CREATE TABLE sales_test
   ( prod_id         NUMBER(6) primary key
   , cust_id         NUMBER
   , time_id         DATE
   , quantity_sold   NUMBER(3)
   , amount_sold     NUMBER(10,2)
   )
PARTITION BY RANGE (time_id)
```

```
         (PARTITION        SALES_1998        VALUES        LESS        THAN
(TO_DATE('01-JAN-1999','DD-MON-YYYY')),
          PARTITION        SALES_1999        VALUES        LESS        THAN
(TO_DATE('01-JAN-2000','DD-MON-YYYY')),
          PARTITION        SALES_2000        VALUES        LESS        THAN
(TO_DATE('01-JAN-2001','DD-MON-YYYY')),
  PARTITION SALES_2001 VALUES LESS THAN (MAXVALUE)
);
```

```
SQL>
SQL> CREATE TABLE sales_test
    ( prod_id        NUMBER(6) primary key
    , cust_id        NUMBER
    , time_id        DATE
    , quantity_sold  NUMBER(3)
    , amount_sold    NUMBER(10,2)
    )
PARTITION BY RANGE (time_id)
  (PARTITION SALES_1998 VALUES LESS THAN (TO_DATE('01-JAN-1999','DD-MON-YYYY')),
   PARTITION SALES_1999 VALUES LESS THAN (TO_DATE('01-JAN-2000','DD-MON-YYYY')),
   PARTITION SALES_2000 VALUES LESS THAN (TO_DATE('01-JAN-2001','DD-MON-YYYY')),
   PARTITION SALES_2001 VALUES LESS THAN (MAXVALUE)
);  2    3    4    5    6    7    8    9   10   11   12   13

Table created.
```

Import Data into New Partition Table

```
# imp file=sales_new.exp tables=sales_new ignore=y
```

```
[oracle@ahmed ~]$
[oracle@ahmed ~]$ imp file=sales_test.dmp tables=sales_test ignore=y

Import: Release 11.2.0.1.0 - Production on Fri Mar 11 07:18:40 2016

Copyright (c) 1982, 2009, Oracle and/or its affiliates.  All rights reserved.

Username: part
Password:

Connected to: Oracle Database 11g Enterprise Edition Release 11.2.0.1.0 - 64bit Production
With the Partitioning, OLAP, Data Mining and Real Application Testing options

Export file created by EXPORT:V11.02.00 via conventional path
import done in US7ASCII character set and AL16UTF16 NCHAR character set
import server uses WE8MSWIN1252 character set (possible charset conversion)
. importing PART's objects into PART
. importing PART's objects into PART
. . importing table                  "SALES_TEST"           10 rows imported
Import terminated successfully without warnings.
```

Again Check if it has become Partition Table or not

```
SQL> select TABLE_NAME,CLUSTER_NAME,PARTITIONED from user_tables;
```

```
SQL>
SQL> select TABLE_NAME,CLUSTER_NAME,PARTITIONED from user_tables;

TABLE_NAME                        CLUSTER_NAME                   PAR
--------------------------------  -----------------------------  ---
TIME_RANGE_SALES                                                 YES
SALES_TEST                                                       YES
SALES_TEST_BKP                                                   NO
```

Drop the Old Table

```
DROP TABLE SALES_NEW_BKP;
```

Verify Data from Partition Tables

```
select * from SALES_TEST partition (SALES_1998);
```

```
SQL>
SQL> select * from SALES_Test partition (SALES_1998);

   PROD_ID    CUST_ID TIME_ID    QUANTITY_SOLD AMOUNT_SOLD
   -------    ------- -------    ------------- -----------
       116      11393 05-JUN-99             1         100
        40     100530 30-NOV-98             1         200
       118        133 06-JUN-01             2         300
        36       4523 27-JAN-99             1         500
       125       9417 04-FEB-98             1         600
        30        170 23-FEB-01             1         700
        24      11899 26-JAN-99             1         800
        45       9491 28-AUG-98             1         100

8 rows selected.
```

```
select * from SALES_NEW partition (SALES_1999);
Select * from SALES_NEW partition (SALES_2000);
select * from SALES_NEW partition (SALES_2001);
SELECT * FROM SALES_NEW;
```

Method 2: Split and Exchange Partition

Let us first create a test table for this activity:

```
CREATE TABLE my_table (
  ID NUMBER,
  description  VARCHAR2(50)

  );
```

```
SQL> CREATE TABLE my_table (
  id              NUMBER,
  description   VARCHAR2(50)
); 2    3    4

Table created.
```

```
INSERT INTO my_table (id, description) VALUES (1, 'One');
INSERT INTO my_table (id, description) VALUES (2, 'Two');
INSERT INTO my_table (id, description) VALUES (3, 'Three');
INSERT INTO my_table (id, description) VALUES (4, 'Four');
COMMIT;
```

Create a Single Full Partition Table with only one Partition to contain whole Table

```
CREATE TABLE my_table_2 (
  ID NUMBER,
  description  VARCHAR2(50)
)
PARTITION BY RANGE (id)
(PARTITION my_table_part VALUES LESS THAN (MAXVALUE));
```

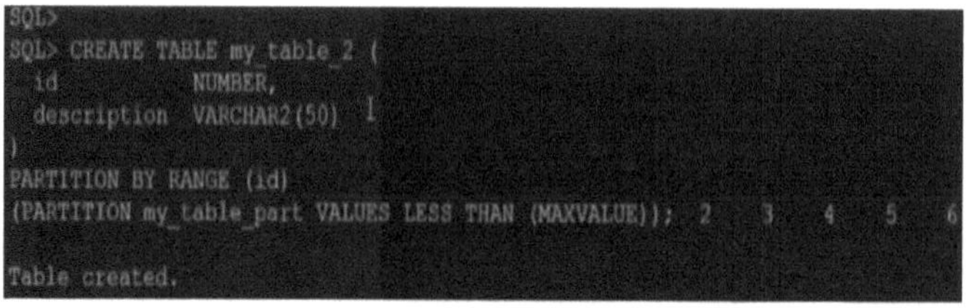

```
SQL>
SQL> CREATE TABLE my_table_2 (
  id            NUMBER,
  description   VARCHAR2(50)
)
PARTITION BY RANGE (id)
(PARTITION my_table_part VALUES LESS THAN (MAXVALUE));  2    3    4    5    6

Table created.
```

Switch Original Table Segment with Partition Table Segment

```
ALTER TABLE my_table_2
  EXCHANGE PARTITION my_table_part
  WITH TABLE my_table
  WITHOUT VALIDATION;
```

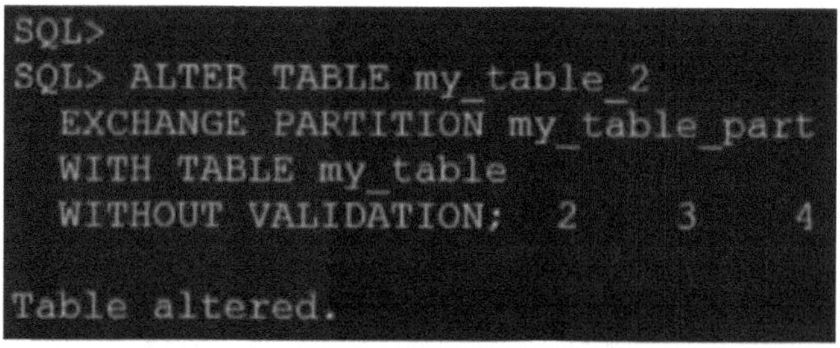

```
SQL>
SQL> ALTER TABLE my_table_2
  EXCHANGE PARTITION my_table_part
  WITH TABLE my_table
  WITHOUT VALIDATION;   2    3    4

Table altered.
```

Drop Original Table and Rename Partition Table

```
DROP TABLE my_table;
```

```
SQL>
SQL> DROP TABLE my_table;

Table dropped.
```

```
RENAME my_table_2 TO my_table;
```

```
SQL>
SQL> RENAME my_table_2 TO my_table;

Table renamed.
```

Finally, We Can Split The New Partition Table Into Multiple Partitions

```
ALTER TABLE my_table SPLIT PARTITION my_table_part AT (3)
INTO (PARTITION my_table_part_1,
      PARTITION my_table_part_2);
```

Check Partition Details

```
SELECT table_name,
       partition_name,
       high_value,
       num_rows
FROM   user_tab_partitions
ORDER BY table_name, partition_name;
```

```
MY_TABLE                          MY_TABLE_PART_1                  3
MY_TABLE                          MY_TABLE_PART_2                  MAXVALUE
SALES_TEST                        SALES_1998                       TO_DATE(' 1999-01-01 00:00:00', 'SYYYY-MM-DD HH24:MI:SS', 'NLS_CALENDAR=
GREGORIA
SALES_TEST                        SALES_1999                       TO_DATE(' 2000-01-01 00:00:00', 'SYYYY-MM-DD HH24:MI:SS', 'NLS_CALENDAR=
GREGORIA
SALES_TEST                        SALES_2000                       TO_DATE(' 2001-01-01 00:00:00', 'SYYYY-MM-DD HH24:MI:SS', 'NLS_CALENDAR=
GREGORIA
SALES_TEST                        SALES_2001                       MAXVALUE
TIME_RANGE_SALES                  SALES_1998                       TO_DATE(' 1999-01-01 00:00:00', 'SYYYY-MM-DD HH24:MI:SS', 'NLS_CALENDAR=
GREGORIA
TIME_RANGE_SALES                  SALES_1999                       TO_DATE(' 2000-01-01 00:00:00', 'SYYYY-MM-DD HH24:MI:SS', 'NLS_CALENDAR=
GREGORIA
TIME_RANGE_SALES                  SALES_2000                       TO_DATE(' 2001-01-01 00:00:00', 'SYYYY-MM-DD HH24:MI:SS', 'NLS_CALENDAR=
GREGORIA
TIME_RANGE_SALES                  SALES_2001                       MAXVALUE

10 rows selected.

SQL>
SQL>
SQL> select * from my_table partition (my_table_part_1);

        ID DESCRIPTION
---------- --------------------------------------------------
         1 One
         2 Two

SQL> select * from my_table partition (my_table_part_2);

        ID DESCRIPTION
---------- --------------------------------------------------
         3 Three
         4 Four
```

Thankyou!

Your comments encourage us to produce quality content, please take a second and say 'Hi' to me and let me and my team know what you thought of the book … p.s. It would mean the world to me if you send a quick email to me ;)

Email: support@dbagenesis.com

- Link to full course: https://dbagenesis.com/
- Link to all DBA courses: https://dbagenesis.com/courses
- Link to real-time projects: https://dbagenesis.com/p/projects
- Link to support articles: https://support.dbagenesis.com

DBA Genesis provides all you need to build and manage effective Oracle technology learning. We designed DBA Genesis as a simple to use yet powerful online Oracle learning system for students. Each of our courses is taught by an expert instructor, and every course is available with a challenging project to push you out of your comfort zone!!

DBA Genesis is currently the fastest & the most engaging learning platforms for DBAs across the globe. Take your database administration skills to next level by enrolling into your first course.

Follow us on Social Media:

- Facebook: https://www.facebook.com/dbagenesis/
- Instagram: https://www.instagram.com/dbagenesis/
- Twitter: https://twitter.com/DbaGenesis
- Website: https://dbagenesis.com/
- Contact us: https://dbagenesis.com/p/contact

All the best and goodbye for now!

Arun Kumar

Notes